DIRT BIKE RACING

BY DALTON RAINS

Copyright © 2024 by Apex Editions, Mendota Heights, MN 55120. All rights reserved. No part of this book may be reproduced or utilized in any form or by any means without written permission from the publisher.

Apex is distributed by North Star Editions:
sales@northstareditions.com | 888-417-0195

Produced for Apex by Red Line Editorial.

Photographs ©: Shutterstock Images, cover, 1, 6, 8–9, 12, 14, 15, 16–17, 22–23, 24–25, 29; Bryan Lynn/Icon Sportswire, 4–5; iStockphoto, 10–11, 21, 26, 27; 400ex127/Dreamstime, 18–19; Eli Hartman/Odessa American/AP Images, 20

Library of Congress Control Number: 2022923637

ISBN
978-1-63738-535-7 (hardcover)
978-1-63738-589-0 (paperback)
978-1-63738-695-8 (ebook pdf)
978-1-63738-643-9 (hosted ebook)

Printed in the United States of America
Mankato, MN
082023

NOTE TO PARENTS AND EDUCATORS

Apex books are designed to build literacy skills in striving readers. Exciting, high-interest content attracts and holds readers' attention. The text is carefully leveled to allow students to achieve success quickly. Additional features, such as bolded glossary words for difficult terms, help build comprehension.

TABLE OF CONTENTS

CHAPTER 1

READY TO RACE

Dirt bike riders line up at the starting gates. They **rev** their engines. The race is about to start.

Racers wait until they see a green flag.
Then they can go.

The gates drop, and the riders speed onto the track. Dust and mud fly up. The riders swerve around corners and bounce over jumps.

FAST FACT

Most dirt bikes can reach speeds of 60 miles per hour (97 km/h).

Riders often stand up during jumps. That helps them land.

7

The riders reach the final **lap**. One rider gets to the inside of a turn. He pulls ahead and crosses the finish line. He wins!

Making tight turns can help racers pass other riders.

TRACKS AND LAPS

In some types of dirt bike racing, riders do several laps around a short track. Other races are long-distance. Riders complete the course just one time.

CHAPTER 2

DiRT BiKE HiSTORY

There are many styles of dirt bike racing. One of the most popular is motocross. It began in the early 1900s.

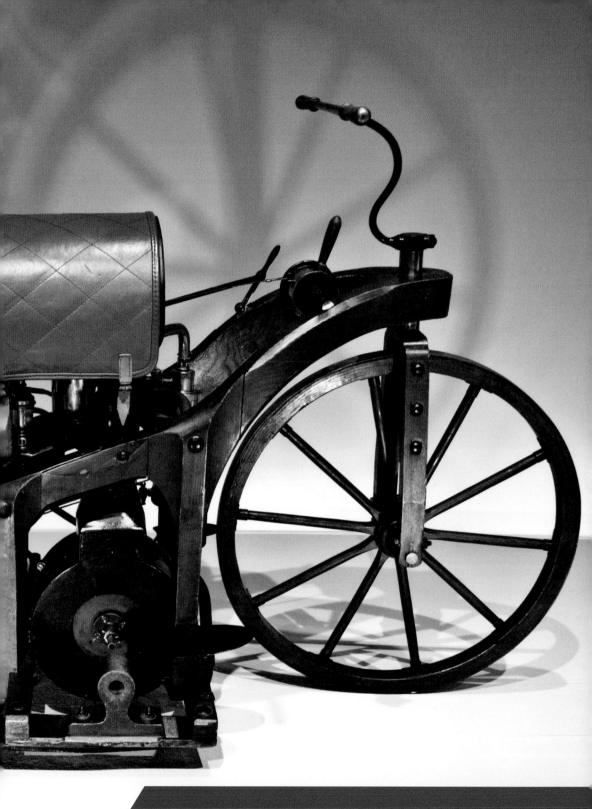

Motorcycles were invented in the 1880s. People began racing them soon after.

Motocross started in the United Kingdom. People held **off-road** motorcycle races. Later, they used dirt tracks. By the 1950s, this kind of racing had spread to the United States.

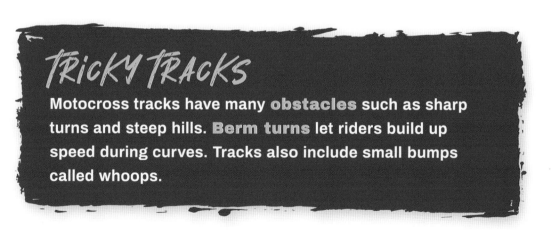

TRICKY TRACKS

Motocross tracks have many **obstacles** such as sharp turns and steep hills. **Berm turns** let riders build up speed during curves. Tracks also include small bumps called whoops.

Each motocross track has a different pattern of hills, jumps, and curves.

Supercross events happen indoors instead of outdoors.

In the 1970s, dirt bike racing continued to grow. New styles like enduro and Supercross started. They used different lengths and types of tracks.

FAST FACT

Some riders do freestyle motocross (FMX). Instead of racing, they do tricks.

Dangerous jumps are some of the tricks that FMX riders perform.

CHAPTER 3

ALL KINDS OF RACES

Each style of dirt bike racing has its own rules and courses. Enduro races are very long. Their tracks include rough **terrain**. Racers ride around trees and through creeks.

Enduro races can last up to seven hours. Some tracks are 150 miles (241 km) long.

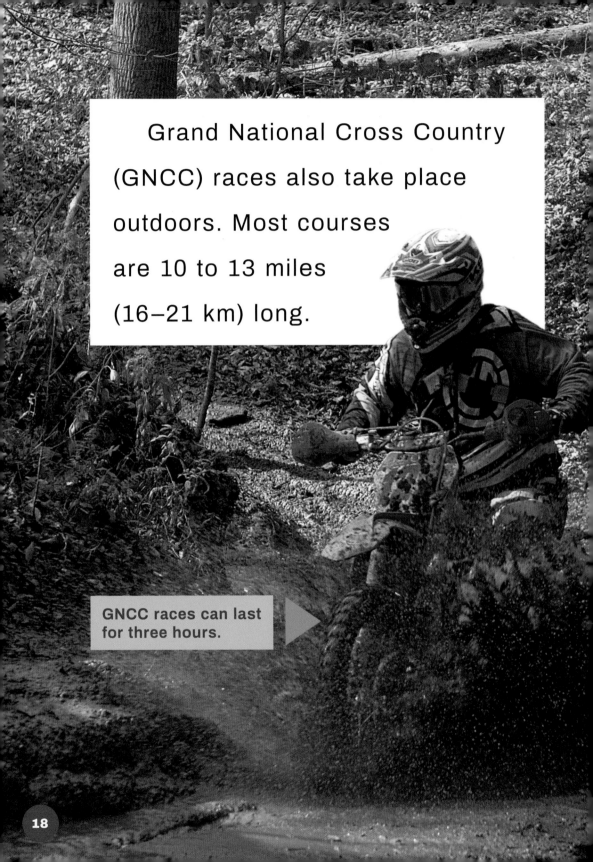

Grand National Cross Country (GNCC) races also take place outdoors. Most courses are 10 to 13 miles (16–21 km) long.

GNCC races can last for three hours.

FAST FACT

Some GNCC races have more than 2,000 riders. They are divided into groups called classes.

Arenacross blends parts of motocross and FMX.

Supercross and Arenacross are indoor events. Their tracks are inside **stadiums** and **arenas**. They often have high jumps.

ENDUROCROSS

EnduroCross is a blend of two other styles. Its tracks are built in arenas. But they have off-road obstacles such as logs, rocks, and water. The tracks also have big jumps.

EnduroCross tracks are indoors. But they have obstacles similar to outdoor enduros.

CHAPTER 4

TYPES OF BIKES

Riders can use different kinds of bikes. It depends on the racing style. Most dirt bikes have powerful engines. Their thick tires grip the ground.

Knobs on a dirt bike's tires help them grip the ground.

Enduro courses can be tough. So, enduro bikes are built to be strong. Their frames and **suspensions** are built to go over bumps.

FAST FACT

Enduro bikes have skid plates. These parts go under the engine to protect it.

Enduro bikes are made to be good at going downhill.

Many dirt bikes weigh about 215 pounds (98 kg).

Motocross bikes also have strong frames and engines. But these bikes are lighter. That helps them move faster.

SUIT UP

Dirt bike racing can be dangerous. So, riders wear helmets and goggles. Riders also wear body pads. This equipment helps keep them safe if they crash.

Goggles protect a rider's eyes from dirt, mud, and bright sunlight.

COMPREHENSION
QUESTIONS

Write your answers on a separate piece of paper.

1. Write a few sentences that explain the main ideas of Chapter 4.

2. Which style of dirt bike racing would you most like to try? Why?

3. Which style of dirt bike racing takes place indoors?

   A. Supercross
   B. motocross
   C. enduro

4. How is EnduroCross similar to Arenacross?

   A. Both styles take place outdoors.
   B. Both styles have indoor tracks with big jumps.
   C. Both styles have indoor tracks with no obstacles.

5. What does **equipment** mean in this book?

*Riders also wear body pads. This **equipment** helps keep them safe if they crash.*

    A. things people take apart

    B. things people use or wear

    C. things people cannot see

6. What does **swerve** mean in this book?

*The riders **swerve** around corners and bounce over jumps.*

    A. move in a curve

    B. go backwards

    C. stop moving

Answer key on page 32.

GLOSSARY

arenas
Large indoor areas where people watch sports or events.

berm turns
Turns where the track is slanted up at the sides.

lap
One loop around a racetrack.

obstacles
Things that block a rider's way.

off-road
Not on a paved road, but often on rough ground instead.

rev
To make an engine speed up and work harder.

stadiums
Huge buildings where people can watch sports or events.

suspensions
Systems on cars or bikes that protect people from feeling hard road or ground conditions.

terrain
An area of land and its physical features.

BOOKS

Amstutz, Lisa J. *The Gearhead's Guide to Dirt Bikes*. North Mankato, MN: Capstone Press, 2023.

O'Neal, Ciara. *Motocross*. Mendota Heights, MN: Apex Editions, 2022.

Shaffer, Lindsay. *Dirt Bikes*. Minneapolis: Bellwether Media, 2019.

ONLINE RESOURCES

Visit **www.apexeditions.com** to find links and resources related to this title.

ABOUT THE AUTHOR

Dalton Rains is a writer and editor from St. Paul, Minnesota. He loves spending time outdoors and learning about all kinds of sports.

INDEX

ANSWER KEY:
1. Answers will vary; 2. Answers will vary; 3. A; 4. B; 5. B; 6. A